NATURAL DISASTERS

Jillian Powell

Editorial Consultants

Adria Klein

Cliff Moon

Lorraine Petersen

Frances Ridley

HAMERAY
PUBLISHING GROUP

Published in the United States of America
by the Hameray Publishing Group, Inc.

Text © Rising Stars UK Ltd.

Published 2008

Author: Jillian Powell
Editorial Consultants: Adria Klein, Cliff Moon,
Lorraine Petersen, and Frances Ridley

Cover design: Button plc
Cover image: Alamy
Text design and typesetting: Andy Wilson
Publisher: Gill Budgell
Project management and editorial: Lesley Densham
Editing: Clare Robertson
Technical adviser: Mandy Holloway (NHM)
Illustrations: Chris King: pages 22–23, 30–31, 36–39
Oxford Illustrators and Designers: pages 13, 14, 27
Photos: Alamy: pages 4–5, 7, 10, 14–15, 19, 20, 25, 32, 35,
40, 41, 43
Corbis: pages 6, 9, 19, 24–25, 28, 29, 35, 43
Getty Images: pages 8, 11, 12, 13, 15, 16–17, 18, 21, 26–27,
33, 41, 42, 43,
Kobal: page 34,
TopFoto: pages 6–7
iStockphoto: page 43

ISBN 978-1-60559-011-0

Printed in China.

1 2 3 4 5 PP 12 11 10 09 08

Contents

The Power of Nature

Earthquakes and volcanoes shake the earth.

Hurricanes and tsunamis destroy cities and kill thousands.

These natural disasters show us the power of nature.

Disaster fact!

There are almost 400 natural disasters every year.

Famous Natural Disasters

Some natural disasters go down in history.

Pompeii

In 79 AD, Mount Vesuvius in Italy erupted. It buried the town of Pompeii under piles of ash.

Everyone living there was killed.

Krakatoa

The volcano Krakatoa exploded in 1883. It destroyed an island in Indonesia.

The blast had the force of a million atomic bombs.

It sent out an ash cloud 50 miles high and a tsunami with over 100 foot high waves.

San Francisco

In 1906, a massive earthquake rocked San Francisco.

The San Andreas fault ripped open for over 300 miles.

The quake sparked fires that burned for three days.

Thousands died or were made homeless.

Meet the Experts

Scientists try to predict natural disasters. They use **sensors**, **radars** and **satellites** to collect data.

Scientists study the patterns of **seismic waves** and compare them to those recorded on previous occasions.

Then the scientists feed the data into a computer.

This is a computer model of a tsunami. It helps scientists to predict whether the tsunami will reach the land.

Animals may be experts too. Some scientists think animals can sense natural disasters before they happen. But there is no proof.

Elephants screamed and ran for higher ground before the tsunami in Indonesia in 2004.

Emergency Teams

Emergency teams are trained to deal with natural disasters. They travel into disaster areas to save lives.

Search and Rescue Teams

Search and rescue teams search for people trapped after earthquakes and other disasters.

They work with dogs and robots. They use **infrared cameras** to help them find people.

Aid Agencies

Aid agencies set up tents and emergency hospitals to treat the injured.

They send in food, water, clothes and blankets.
They help to reunite families.

The Army

Armies bring in emergency aid by road and air.

They help to rescue survivors.

Earthquakes

Earthquakes can destroy whole cities.
They can cause landslides and tsunamis.

Earthquake fact!

The world's biggest earthquake in recent years happened in Chile in 1960.

How do they happen?

Earth's crust is made up of plates, or layers of rock. The plates meet at **fault lines**.

Sometimes the plates clash together and cause an earthquake.

The place where this happens is called the epicenter.

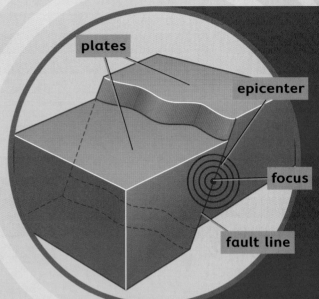

plates

epicenter

focus

fault line

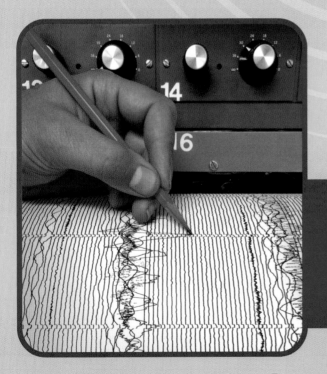

Scientists measure earthquakes on a **seismometer**.

Tsunamis

A tsunami is a giant wave.

Tsunami waves can be 125 miles long. They can travel hundreds of miles and reach speeds of up to 500 mph.

Tsunami fact!

Tsunami waves get taller as they reach coastal waters.

How do they happen?

An earthquake lifts part of the seabed. This pushes up vast amounts of water.

Huge waves moved out from the **epicenter**.

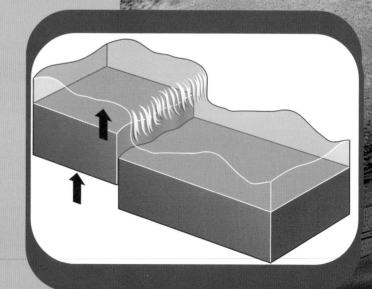

2004 Tsunami

On December 26th, 2004, a huge earthquake rocked the Indian ocean. It caused a tsunami that killed thousands of people.

The Indonesian coastline

Before the tsunami

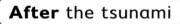

After the tsunami

Case Study: Emergency Aid

A massive tsunami hits south Asia. Over 230,000 people are killed. Thousands more are injured or homeless.

A worldwide aid effort gets under way.

Food, water, shelter, blankets and medicine are sent in ships and planes.

Trucks and helicopters take the aid to the people who need it.

A single air drop can deliver 18 tons of aid.

Volcanoes

Our planet has a core of fire deep under the earth's crust. Sometimes hot rock and gas have to escape. They burst out through volcanoes.

Volcanoes can be dramatic and deadly.

They can bury towns under ash and **lava**.

They can set off tsunamis and black out the sun.

Mount St. Helens in Washington state erupted in 1980. It killed 58 people and caused damage costing $1 billion.

The force of the blast reached over 600 mph. People heard the blast in Canada!

Volcano fact!

Undersea volcanoes sometimes erupt to make new islands.

The deadliest volcanoes of all are under the earth. They are called **supervolcanoes**.

One of the biggest supervolcanoes is under Yellowstone National Park in Wyoming. It erupts about every 600,000 years.

The last eruption was 640,000 years ago!

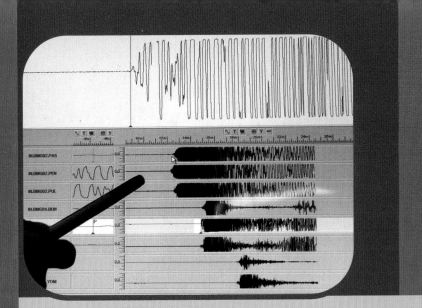

Scientists use instruments to "listen" to active volcanoes.

They take temperature data from **satellites**.

They use **sensors** to "sniff" changes in volcano gases from 12 miles away.

Studying volcanoes can still be a deadly job. In 1993, six scientists were killed in Colombia. They were studying the crater of an active volcano when it suddenly erupted.

Tornado Trouble
(Part One)

"Hurry up, Carl!"

Mr. Thomson sounded a little annoyed now.

Carl was making a volcano and the rest
of the class had finished theirs. But Carl
wanted his to be a supervolcano. He had
built the model and painted it. Now he
just had to put the mix in. What had
Mr. Thomson said? Mix up the soap and
baking soda … pour that in. Now, add the
vinegar and stand back …

BOOM!

Carl's volcano had exploded all over
the classroom.

There were bits of foam on the chalkboard.
There was even a bit on Mr. Thomson's tie.
The whole class was laughing … except for
Mr. Thomson. He looked like he would be
the next to explode.

Continued on page 30

Hurricanes

Hurricanes are powerful storms.
They are also called **typhoons** or **cyclones**.

On land, they can destroy trees, cars and houses. They can even wipe out whole cities.

Hurricane facts!

Hurricanes always circle around an **eye**.

Hurricanes are given names in the order of the alphabet.

Scientists can predict the path and strength of a hurricane. They use computers to help them.

Hurricane hunters fly aircraft into hurricanes to get data.

Tornadoes

A tornado is a tunnel of fast-moving wind. **Tornadoes** are also called **twisters**. They can suck up cows and cars and make buildings explode.

How do they happen?

1. Warm air and cold air come together.

2. Storm clouds form and start to circle.

3. The warm air gets sucked upwards.

4. It makes a funnel of wind that spins faster and faster.

Tornado fact!

Tornadoes are measured on the Fujita scale from F0 to F5. F5s can reach speeds of over 200 mph and damage concrete buildings.

The United States gets more tornadoes than any other country.

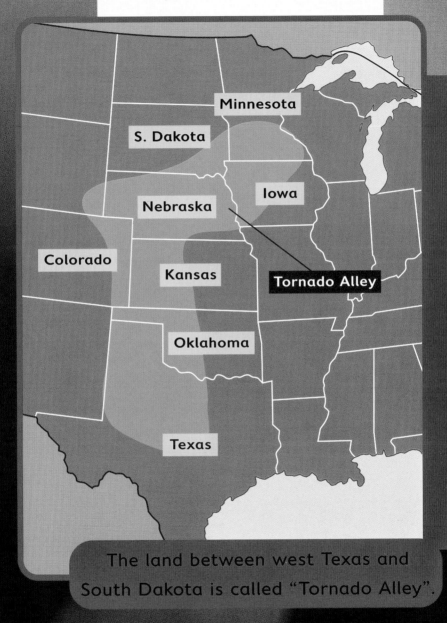

The land between west Texas and South Dakota is called "Tornado Alley".

Floods and Landslides

Floods

Floods can be caused by:

- ◎ heavy rain
- ◎ melting snow
- ◎ rivers bursting their banks
- ◎ **storm surges** on the coast.

Some floods happen without warning.
They are called flash floods.

Hurricane Katrina caused massive flooding in New Orleans in 2005.

Landslides

Landslides can bury villages and kill thousands of people.

A landslide can be caused by rain.

The rain breaks up mud on the mountain side.

Then the mud slides down the mountain.

Tornado Trouble
(Part Two)

Mr. Thomson had not forgotten the volcano episode. He had his eye on Carl.

"Are you listening, Carl?"

"Mm … yes, Mr. Thomson."

Carl was looking out of the window. Something odd was happening out there.

The sky had gone dark. Hail was rattling against the windows. The wind was picking up speed. A paper bag swirled around the playground.

"So what is the difference between a hurricane and a typhoon?"

"A tornado ... I think it's a tornado," Carl muttered.

"Not a tornado!" Mr. Thomson thundered. "We're doing tornadoes next week!"

But Carl wasn't listening. He was watching the huge black cloud. It was getting nearer and nearer.

Continued on page 36

Drought and Forest Fires

Drought

A drought happens when there is no rain for a long time.

The earth cracks, crops don't grow and animals and people die.

Drought can last for months or even years.

Forest Fires

Forests get very dry during a drought. Forest fires start easily and spread quickly.

Natural Disasters at the Movies

Movie heroes often fight natural disasters.

They save the world from destruction.
But could it really happen?

The Core (2003)

Natural disaster The earth has stopped spinning.
This sets off huge electrical storms.

What do they do? Use a massive explosion to
set it spinning again.

Could it happen? Scientists don't think the Earth
will ever stop spinning.

Armageddon (1995)

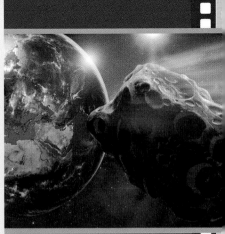

Natural disaster An **asteroid** the size of Texas is about to collide with Earth.

What do they do? Drill a hole in the asteroid. Then blast it apart with explosives.

Could it happen? Yes, but asteroids this big only come around every 50 to 100 million years!

The Day After Tomorrow (2004)

Natural disaster The polar ice caps have melted. This causes massive storms and a new ice age.

What do they do? Go into hiding until the storms blow over.

Could it happen? Climate change *is* happening — but over years, not days, as in the movie.

Tornado Trouble
(Part Three)

"Mr. Thomson! It's a tornado … and it's coming towards us!"

Carl jumped up, pointing out of the window.

"Oh yes, very funny," Mr. Thomson said. "The only tornado in this classroom is …"

CRASH!

Carl looked outside.

The sky was completely black. The great
black cloud was swirling like a funnel.
It was sucking up everything in its path.

A trash can flew past the window.
Bricks and tiles fell out of the sky.
Car alarms screamed.

"Everybody down!" Mr. Thomson shouted.
"Get under the desks!"

Continued on the next page

The school shook. The windows smashed. Bits of glass went flying.

It lasted less than a minute. Then the sky got brighter and the noise stopped.

Everyone stood up. They looked out through the jagged windows.

The fence had been flattened. A car had been lifted up and dropped by the gates. The wall of the science room had been ripped off. You could see the desks inside.

"Everybody all right?" Mr. Thomson looked shaken.

He looked at his watch. "10:54," he said. "And I think we have just had our very own tornado."

"Looks like we're doing tornadoes this week after all!" whispered Carl.

Future Fears

Giant Asteroids

Some asteroids are more than a mile across.

If one hit the sea, it would cause a huge tsunami.

Supervolcanoes

If a supervolcano erupted, its ash would blot out the sun. Earth's climate would change overnight.

Supervolcanoes could even make us extinct!

Solar Flares

A giant **solar flare** could knock out our computers and phones. It could leave planet Earth without power.

Mega-Tsunamis

A massive landslide in the Canary Islands could trigger a mega-tsunami.

The giant wave would destroy the east coast of America.

Global Warming

Global warming is the biggest natural disaster we face today. It is caused by carbon gases from cars and industry which are warming up the planet.

A 3°F to 6°F rise in the next century could spell disaster.

Polar ice caps and glaciers melt.

Sea levels rise, leaving 200 million people homeless.

Crops fail because of drought.

40% of species become extinct.

What would happen?

Violent storms increase.

Quiz

1. What happened to Pompeii in 79 AD?

2. What can seismic signals help predict?

3. What causes most tsunamis?

4. What are hurricanes also called?

5. What do hurricanes circle around?

6. What is another name for tornadoes?

7. How are tornadoes measured?

8. What is a supervolcano?

9. Where is one of the biggest supervolcanoes located?

10. How might a giant solar flare affect life on Earth?

Glossary of Terms

asteroid	A rocky piece of debris in space
cyclone	Another name for a hurricane
earthquake	When the earth's rocks suddenly crack and release shock waves
epicenter	The center of an earthquake
eye	A calm center which usually develops at the core of a hurricane
fault line	The lines that show that there has been movement in the earth's crust
hurricane	A storm, often tropical, with a powerful wind
infrared cameras	They reveal warm areas where people are or have been
lava	Hot, liquid rock that flows out from a volcano
radar	Instrument that detects objects by sending out energy waves
satellite	An object that orbits the Earth, collecting data
seismic waves	Shock waves that travel through the earth and can help us to predict volcanic eruptions
seismometer	An instrument that measures seismic signals
sensor	Instrument that picks up changes in humidity, temperature and other data
solar flare	An explosive release of gases and radiation from the Sun
storm surge	A sudden increase in size and power of waves at sea, caused by storms
supervolcano	A large underground volcano
tornado	A tunnel of very fast-moving wind
tsunami	A giant wave
twister	Another name for a tornado
typhoon	Another name for a hurricane
volcano	A hole, usually in a mountain, from which hot rock and gases erupt from deep beneath the earth's surface

More Resources

Books

Natural Disasters
Clare Watts and Trevor Day
Published by DK Children
(ISBN-10:0756620724; ISBN-13:978-0756620721)
An in-depth look into all kinds of natural disasters.

Violent Volcanoes and Earth-shattering Earthquakes (Horrible Geography)
Anita Ganeri
Published by Scholastic
(ISBN-10:0439950074; ISBN-13:978-0439950077)
An entertaining look at some of nature's nastiest tricks.

Websites

www.phschool.com/science/planetdiary
An up-to-the-minute diary of natural disasters as they happen around the world.

www.library.thinkquest.org/16132/frames.html
Information on all kinds of natural disasters.

DVDs

National Geographic's Nature's Fury (2004)
Scientific explanations and video of natural disasters make this movie a must see!

National Geographic's Forces of Nature (2004)
Tornadoes, tsunamis, and volcanoes – and some cutting edge computer graphics that show the science of natural disasters.

Answers

1. It was destroyed by the eruption of Mount Vesuvius.

2. Volcanoes and earthquakes

3. Undersea earthquakes

4. Typhoons or cyclones

5. An eye

6. Twisters

7. On the Fujita scale 0F – 5F

8. A giant underground volcano

9. Under Yellowstone Park in Wyoming

10. It could knock out computers and phones and leave us without power.

Index